# Dalai Lama

# CHERRY LAKE PRESS

Published in the United States of America by Cherry Lake Publishing Group
Ann Arbor, Michigan
www.cherrylakepublishing.com

Reading Adviser: Marla Conn, MS Ed., Literacy specialist, Read-Ability, Inc.
Book Designer: Jennifer Wahi
Illustrator: Jeff Bane

Photo Credits: ©beibaoke/shutterstock, 5; ©matkub2499/shutterstock, 7; ©Public Domain/Wikimedia, 9; ©Public Domain/Wikimedia/Brooke Dolan and Ilya Tolstoy, 11; ©Richard Mortel/flickr, 13; ©Public Domain/flickr/Lha Socialwork, 15, 22; ©StepanPopov/shutterstock, 17, 23; ©ChameleonsEye/shutterstock, 19; ©Chaton Chokpatara/shutterstock, 21; Jeff Bane, Cover, 1, 6, 10, 18

Library of Congress Cataloging-in-Publication Data

Names: Pincus, Meeg, author. | Bane, Jeff, 1957- illustrator.
Title: Dalai Lama / Meeg Pincus ; illustrated by Jeff Bane.
Description: Ann Arbor, Michigan : Cherry Lake Publishing, [2021] | Series: My itty-bitty bio | Includes index. | Audience: Grades K-1 | Summary: "The My Itty-Bitty Bio series are biographies for the earliest readers. This book examines the life of the Dalai Lama, the 14th spiritual leader of the Tibetan people, in a simple, age-appropriate way that will help young readers develop word recognition and reading skills. Includes a table of contents, author biography, timeline, glossary, index, and other informative backmatter"-- Provided by publisher.
Identifiers: LCCN 2020036008 (print) | LCCN 2020036009 (ebook) | ISBN 9781534179943 (hardcover) | ISBN 9781534181656 (paperback) | ISBN 9781534180956 (pdf) | ISBN 9781534182660 (ebook)
Subjects: LCSH: Bstan-'dzin-rgya-mtsho, Dalai Lama XIV, 1935---Juvenile literature. | Dalai lamas--Biography--Juvenile literature. | Tibet Region--Biography.
Classification: LCC BQ7935.B777 P56 2021 (print) | LCC BQ7935.B777 (ebook) | DDC 294.3/923092 [B]--dc23
LC record available at https://lccn.loc.gov/2020036008
LC ebook record available at https://lccn.loc.gov/2020036009

Printed in the United States of America
Corporate Graphics

APRIL 2021

**About the author:** Meeg Pincus has been a writer, editor, and educator for 25 years. She loves to write inspiring stories for kids about people, animals, and our planet. She lives near San Diego, California, where she enjoys the beach, reading, singing, and her family.

**About the illustrator:** Jeff Bane and his two business partners own a studio along the American River in Folsom, California, home of the 1849 Gold Rush. When Jeff's not sketching or illustrating for clients, he's either swimming or kayaking in the river to relax.

I was born in a small **village** in Tibet. It was 1935. I had many brothers and sisters.

My parents were **Buddhists**.
They taught me **compassion** for
all living things. We lived simply.

Buddhist leaders visited our home. I was 2. They said I was born to lead Tibet.

I went to live with Buddhist **monks**. I was taught many subjects. I learned about art and **medicine**.

What do you like to learn?

I became the leader of Tibet.
I was 15.

China took over Tibet. It was **violent**. I was 24. I escaped to India. I still live there today.

I work with world leaders. I want peace for all.

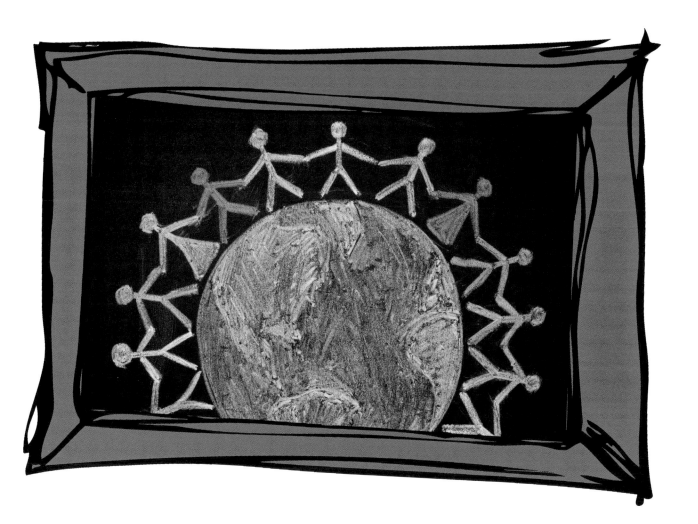

I travel around the world. I give talks. I write many books.

What do you like to do?

I **stepped down** as Tibet's leader. I was 76 years old. I am loved as a Buddhist teacher. I work to bring peace to the world.

What would you like to ask me?

1959

1930

Born
1935

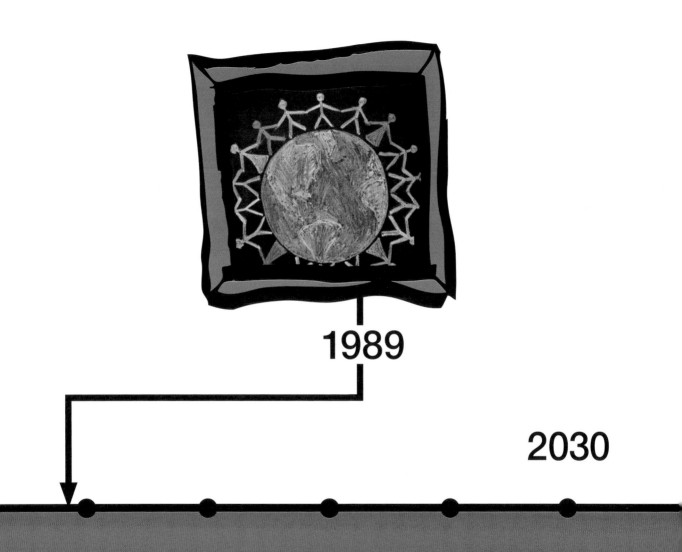

1989

2030

23

## glossary

**Buddhists** (BOO-dists) people who practice the teachings of Buddha, who lived around 500 BCE

**compassion** (kuhm-PASH-uhn) understanding someone who is suffering and wanting to help them

**medicine** (MED-ih-sihn) the study and treatment of diseases and injuries

**monks** (MUHNGKS) men who live apart from society in a religious community with strict rules

**stepped down** (STEPD DOUN) left a position of leadership

**village** (VIL-ij) a place where people live that is smaller than a town

**violent** (VYE-uh-luhnt) harmful by physical force

## index

24